Words of Life
Youth Study Book

WORDS OF LIFE
JESUS AND THE PROMISE OF THE TEN COMMANDMENTS TODAY

Words of Life: Jesus and the Promise of the Ten Commandments Today
978-1-5247-6054-0 *Hardcover*
978-1-5247-6055-7 *eBook*
978-0-5932-0828-1 *Audio*

Words of Life: DVD
978-1-7910-1326-4

Words of Life: Leader Guide
978-1-7910-1324-0
978-1-7910-1325-7 eBook

Words of Life: Youth Study Book
978-1-7910-1333-2
978-1-7910-1334-9 eBook

Words of Life: Children's Leader Guide
978-1-7910-1335-6

Also by Adam Hamilton

24 Hours That Changed the World
Christianity and World Religions
Christianity's Family Tree
Confronting the Controversies
Creed
Enough
Faithful
Final Words from the Cross
Forgiveness
Half Truths
Incarnation
John
Leading Beyond the Walls
Love to Stay
Making Sense of the Bible
Moses

Not a Silent Night
Revival
Seeing Gray in a World of Black and White
Selling Swimsuits in the Arctic
Simon Peter
Speaking Well
The Call
The Journey
The Walk
The Way
Unafraid
Unleashing the Word
When Christians Get It Wrong
Why?

For more information, visit www.AdamHamilton.com.

Words of Life

Jesus and the Promise of the Ten Commandments Today

Adam Hamilton

Bestselling Author of *Making Sense of the Bible*

YOUTH STUDY BOOK
by Josh Tinley

Abingdon Press | Nashville

**Words of Life
Jesus and the Promise
of the Ten Commandments Today
Youth Study Book**

Copyright © 2020 Abingdon Press
All rights reserved.

No part of this work may be reproduced or transmitted in any form or by any means, electronic or mechanical, including photocopying and recording, or by any information storage or retrieval system, except as may be expressly permitted by the 1976 Copyright Act or in writing from the publisher. Requests for permission can be addressed to Permissions, The United Methodist Publishing House, 2222 Rosa L. Parks Blvd., Nashville, TN 37228-1306 or e-mailed to permissions@umpublishing.org.

978-1-7910-1333-2

Unless noted otherwise, Scripture quotations are taken from the Common English Bible, copyright 2011. Used by permission. All rights reserved.

Scriptures noted KJV are from The Authorized (King James) Version. Rights in the Authorized Version in the United Kingdom are vested in the Crown. Reproduced by permission of the Crown's patentee, Cambridge University Press.

20 21 22 23 24 25 26 27 28 29 — 10 9 8 7 6 5 4 3 2 1
MANUFACTURED IN THE UNITED STATES OF AMERICA

CONTENTS

Introduction 7

Session 1: At the Center of It All 11

Session 2: The Idols We Keep 17

Session 3: "I Swear to God!" 23

Session 4: Rediscovering the Joy of Sabbath 30

Session 5: A Question of Honor 37

Session 6: The Tragedy of Violence, the Beauty of Mercy 45

Session 7: Faithfulness in an Unfaithful Age 51

Session 8: We're All Thieves. Yes, Even You. 57

Session 9: Sticks, Stones, and the Power of Words 63

Session 10: Keeping Up with the Joneses 70

INTRODUCTION

Exodus 20:1-17, better known as the Ten Commandments, is one of the most famous passages in Scripture. This list of instructions, given by God to the ancient Israelites, is displayed in many churches and other religious institutions. There have been heated debates and court cases involving whether the commandments should be posted in public places. The 1956 movie *The Ten Commandments*, directed by Cecil B. DeMille and starring Charlton Heston, won seven Academy Awards (including Best Picture) and was one of the most financially successful movies in history.

Most people know *of* the Ten Commandments, but fewer actually know the commandments themselves. A 2007 survey by Kelton Research found that Americans were more familiar with the members of The Brady Bunch (from the sitcom that ran from 1969 to 1974) and the ingredients of McDonald's Big Mac than with the Ten Commandments. Fewer than sixty percent of the people surveyed knew that "Do not kill" was one of the Ten Commandments; only 34 percent knew that there was a commandment involving the Sabbath; and only 29 percent knew that there was a commandment involving idols.[1]

Relatively few people know all of the commandments. Even fewer really understand them. The Ten Commandments are the first of the laws that God sent to the ancient Israelites as part of the covenant God made with them on Mount Sinai. These laws gave the Israelites instructions on how to treat one another, how to interact with their neighbors, how to handle disputes, how to make sure everyone is cared for, and how to set themselves apart as God's people.

The commandments were originally written in ancient Hebrew, a language that doesn't always translate smoothly into English. So we

---

[1] "Americans Know Big Macs Better Than Ten Commandments," Reuters, October 12, 2007, https://www.reuters.com/article/us-bible-commandments/americans-know-big-macs-better-than-ten-commandments-idUSN1223894020071012.

have a list of instructions written to address the challenges and struggles of an ancient culture in another part of the world in a language very different from our own. Yet, when we look closely, we find that the Ten Commandments are just as relevant for us in twenty-first-century North America as they were for the ancient Israelites.

About This Study

This study for youth examines each of the Ten Commandments. It looks at the wording of the commandments and what they meant to the people who first wrote them and heard them. It considers what Jesus has to say about these commandments and what they mean for his followers. And it explores how these ancient teachings apply to our modern world.

This study includes ten sessions, one session for each commandment. You can do this study in one of several ways, depending on the length of time you want to focus on the study.

Ten-week study: Do one session (one commandment) each week. Some sessions may have more activities than you can fit into your meeting time. If time becomes a problem, review the activities in advance and choose which ones you want to do.

Five-week study: Do two sessions (two commandments) each week.

Six-week study: Follow the plan below, choosing the activities from each session that you want to focus on.

- *Week 1:* Sessions 1 and 2
- *Week 2:* Sessions 3 and 4
- *Week 3:* Session 5
- *Week 4:* Sessions 6 and 7
- *Week 5:* Sessions 8 and 9
- *Week 6:* Session 10

Each session includes the following:

- an opening activity and prayer. Participants will do a fun activity while waiting for everyone to arrive. This activity will introduce that session's commandment;

Introduction

- a variety of teaching and learning activities and discussion questions; and
- a closing review and prayer.

Every session plan and activity includes a list of necessary supplies. You also may want to invite participants to have a notebook, journal, or electronic tablet for use during this study. Explain that these can be used to record questions and insights they have as they read each chapter and to take notes during each session.

The primary supplies you will need for this study are:

- this book,
- Bibles,
- paper and pens or pencils,
- a whiteboard or large sheets of paper,
- markers, and
- devices with internet access.

Note: If you wish to watch the *Words of Life* videos (see page 10) as a part of this study, allow an extra twenty minutes in your meeting session for viewing and discussion. Each video is approximately ten minutes long.

Using This Book

This book acts as both a leader's guide and participant book for the study. Each person in the group, including the leader, should have a copy of this book. Throughout the study, participants will be asked to write or draw in response to questions and prompts.

Your leader may be an adult leader, such as a youth minister or Sunday school teacher. But because of the format, this study is a great opportunity for student leadership. One or two youth participants can take the responsibility of leading the entire study. Or you can do a rotation where a different participant leads each session. Leaders will need to prepare by doing the following:

- reading the session plan and familiarizing themselves with the activities. Depending on the time you have available, leaders may also need to select which activities the group will be doing.

- reading and familiarizing themselves with the scriptures that appear in that session. If possible, participants should look up these scriptures in a study Bible that provides notes and commentary on hard-to-understand verses.
- working with adult leaders to make sure that the group has all the necessary supplies. A supply list is provided at the beginning of each session.

Even if you do a student-led study, be sure to have proper adult supervision (in accordance with your church's safety policies).

Words of Life Book

This study is based on the book *Words of Life: Jesus and the Promise of the Ten Commandments Today*, by Adam Hamilton (Convergent, 2020). The book contains much more in-depth information about the Ten Commandments, Jesus's approach to them, and their relevance for our lives today. Many youth may want to read it on their own or as part of the study, as a way of enriching their faith and understanding.

Words of Life Videos

A *Words of Life* DVD is also available, featuring ten videos of Adam Hamilton discussing the Ten Commandments, taking you on a tour of various locations in Egypt, and holding conversations with Rabbi Arthur Nemitoff about Jewish perspectives on the Ten Commandments. If you wish to watch these videos as part of your study, allow an extra twenty minutes for viewing and discussion (each video is approximately ten minutes long). You may also watch these videos on the Amplify Media platform (www.amplifymedia.com) if your church has a subscription.

Session 1

AT THE CENTER OF IT ALL

You must have no other gods before me.
(Exodus 20:3)

If you think about it, it's a little weird that our name for God is "God." Countless religions have come and gone throughout human history. Very few have referred to their gods using the noun that means "god." Followers of the Abrahamic religions (Christians, Jews, and Muslims, among others) call our god "God," because we believe that there is only one God. We don't need to distinguish our God from any other divine beings.

This wasn't always the case. The ancient Israelites lived in a world where every nation had its own gods. People could be tempted to worship another nation's gods if those gods appeared to be more powerful or generous. Thus, God's first commandment for the Israelites is "I am your only God. You can't worship anybody else's gods."

This doesn't seem to be much of an issue in North America in the twenty-first century. Most people would say that they either worship our God or no god at all. But if we take a closer look, we'll discover that there are other gods. We just don't usually think of them that way. When someone or something captures our attention and devotion to the point that it becomes a bigger priority than our relationship with God, it has become a god.

In this session, we'll visit the world of the ancient Israelites and look at what this commandment meant to them. Then we'll consider some of the gods that we are tempted to worship today.

Getting Ready

For this session you will need:

- Bibles,
- paper and pens or pencils,
- a whiteboard or large sheet of paper,

- markers, and
- paper.

Opening: Can You Name All Ten? (5–10 minutes)

Supplies: Bibles, pens or pencils, paper

As you are waiting for everyone to arrive, write on a sheet of paper as many of the Ten Commandments as you can remember.

When most people are present and have had a chance to list the commandments they can think of, divide into teams of three or four people and make sure each team has a sheet of paper. As a team, combine your lists and see how many total commandments you can come up with.

After a couple minutes, see which team has listed the most commandments (or if any team has listed all ten). This team should read aloud their list. While this team reads, members of other teams should turn to Exodus 20:1-17 and check this team's work.

Note: While pretty much all Christian and Jewish traditions recognize ten commandments from Exodus 20:1-17, Protestants, Catholics, and Jews traditionally identify and number these commandments differently. While this study follows the Protestant list of commandments, we'll also look at the differences among the lists. If there is some disagreement during this activity about what is or is not a commandment, it probably will be resolved later in this study.

Open with the following prayer or one of your choosing:

God, thank you for bringing us together to begin this study of your law and the importance that these ancient teachings still have for us today. Open our hearts and minds to the message that you have for us. Amen.

Setting the Stage (15 minutes)

Supplies: Bibles, pens or pencils

Invite a participant to read aloud the following:

> God gave God's people the Ten Commandments, along with many other laws, toward the beginning of their forty-year journey through the desert wilderness on their way to the Promised Land.

Before getting into the commandments, see if you can put in order the events leading up to God giving the law to the Israelite people. Divide into teams of three or four, then work together to put the following events in order.

- God's people cross the Red Sea to escape slavery on dry land.
- God makes a covenant with Abram and Sarai, later known as Abraham and Sarah.
- Jacob flees from his angry brother, Esau.
- Joseph's brothers sell Joseph into slavery in Egypt.
- God calls Moses to deliver God's people from slavery in Egypt.
- Jacob's family moves to Egypt, where one of Jacob's sons has become an important leader.

When you're finished, check your work by looking up these scriptures:

- Genesis 12:1-3; 17:1-8
- Genesis 27:41–28:5
- Genesis 37:1-28
- Genesis 45:25-28; 47:1-12
- Exodus 3:1-12
- Exodus 14

Wrap up by inviting a participant to read aloud the following:

Safely free from the Egyptian army, the Israelites travel to Mount Sinai, also known as Mount Horeb, where God gives the law to Moses. The Ten Commandments are the first of many laws that will govern the Israelites' life together in the wilderness and, eventually, in the Promised Land.

The First Commandment (5 minutes)

Supplies: Bibles

Ask a volunteer to read aloud Exodus 20:2-3.
Invite a participant to read aloud the following:

*According to Jewish tradition, the first commandment is the statement, "I am the L*ORD *your God who brought you out of Egypt, out of the house of slavery," from verse 2. The second commandment is verse 3, "You must have no other gods before me." But for most Christians, verse 2 is a prelude to the commandments and the first commandment is in verse 3.*

Discuss:

- What do you know about gods and religions in the ancient world?
- When have you believed in something or held an opinion that most of your peers rejected?
- Were you tempted to change this unpopular belief or opinion? Why, or why not?

Invite a participant to read aloud the following:

Monotheism, the worship of one god, was rare in the ancient Mediterranean world. In the 14th century BC, the Egyptian pharaoh Akhenaten decreed that the Egyptian people would worship only one of their many gods, Aten, who was represented by the sun. Akhenaten declared not only that Aten was the greatest of the gods but also that he was the only god. This was a radical change in thinking from what the Egyptians were used to. And after Akhenaten's death, Egypt went back to worshipping many gods. They were embarrassed that they had been worshipping only one god and tried to erase Akhenaten's religion from their historical records. The Israelites, who worshipped only one God for many generations, were unique in their time.

Other Gods? (10–15 minutes)

Supplies: large sheet of paper, markers, pens or pencils

Invite a participant to read aloud:

The first commandment says that we should have no gods before our God, the one true God. The ancient Israelites had many gods competing for their attention and worship. Other nations in the area, including nations that were bigger and more powerful than Israel, had their own gods. We live in a very different world. Most people in the twenty-first-century United States either worship the God of Abraham, like the Israelites, or worship no god at all. What does it mean for us to follow the first commandment?

Take three minutes to brainstorm gods that compete for our attention today. Don't focus on gods who might be worshipped by other religious traditions. Instead, try to identify other things that we might devote our lives to. This could include people, possessions, abstract concepts such as fame or success, or political ideologies, among other things.

As a group, list your ideas on a whiteboard or large sheet of paper. Then discuss:

- Look at the items we listed. Have you ever considered any of these to be gods? If so, which ones?
- If you were to think of these things as gods, how would your life and your decisions change?
- What is one item from the list that you, personally, might be tempted to put before God?

What Is God's Name? (5 minutes)

Supplies: Bibles

Discuss:

- What are some names of gods from other religions and mythologies that you are familiar with?

Invite a participant to read aloud:

> *We often refer to God as "God," which seems a little bit like calling a cat "Cat." If we call God by another name, it is usually a title such as "Lord" or "Father." We don't call God by a name such as "Thor" or "Athena" or "Shiva" or "Larry" or "Barbara." But when God spoke to Moses from the burning bush, Moses asked for God's name. And God answered him.*

Invite a participant to read aloud Exodus 3:13-15.

Discuss:

- According to these verses, what is God's name?
- What does this name tell us about God?
- If you were in Moses's situation what follow-up questions might you have had for God?

Invite a participant to read aloud:

In English translations such as the Common English Bible, God's name in Exodus 3:14 is "I Am" or "I Am Who I Am" or "I Will Be Who I Will Be." But in the ancient Hebrew of the Old Testament, God's name is only four letters, and all of them are consonants: YHWH. We don't know the vowel sounds, and Jewish people traditionally do not speak the name of God because it is sacred. So we don't really know the exact translation or pronunciation of this name. The most common pronunciation is Yahweh.

Closing (5 minutes)

To close, discuss the following questions:

- What is one thing you learned from our time together today that you didn't know before?
- What is one question you have as a result of what we've discussed today?

Close with the following prayer or one of your choosing:

Lord God, our provider and protector, thank you for bringing us together for this time of study and reflection. Thank you for the insights you've given us and the questions you've raised. As we leave here, guide us and strengthen us so that we can resist the temptation to follow other gods and can focus on your will for us. We pray these things in Jesus's name. Amen.

Session 2

THE IDOLS WE KEEP

Do not make an idol for yourself.
(Exodus 20:4)

The famous 1981 movie *Raiders of the Lost Ark* opens with the hero, famed archaeologist Indiana Jones, retrieving an idol from an ancient temple guarded with deadly traps. The idol, which Dr. Jones soon loses to a rival archaeologist, is a small golden statue. The wildly successful 2011 mobile video game, *Temple Run*, involves an explorer escaping from a temple with an idol, an ancient relic similar to the one in *Raiders*.

When we think of idols, we probably think of little golden statues, things that ancient cultures worshipped because they weren't familiar with our God. While the second commandment involves these little golden statues, it also involves much more.

Even those of us who have never made or worshipped little statues have likely been guilty of making idols. We can make an idol out of money or awards or video games or celebrities, or any number of other things. Whenever something becomes more of a priority for us than our relationship with God, it has become an idol. In this session, we'll examine the difference between worshipping an idol and having a relationship with God. We'll also look at the ancient Christian tradition of creating icons.

Getting Ready

For this session you will need:

- Bibles,
- paper and pens or pencils,
- a whiteboard or large sheet of paper,
- markers, and
- devices with internet access.

Opening: Statues (10 minutes)

Supplies: modeling clay or Legos

As participants arrive, invite each person to take some modeling clay or a handful of Lego bricks; then use those materials to build a statue commemorating a person, event, or object that they consider especially important or meaningful.

When most people are present and have had a chance to sculpt, allow each person to show his or her sculpture.

Then discuss:

- What sculptures are prominently displayed in our community or state? What do these sculptures commemorate?
- What is the purpose of putting sculptures of people or events in public areas?
- If you had the opportunity, what people or events would you commemorate with a statue?
- Are there statues that you would prefer be taken down? If so, which statues, and why?

Open with the following prayer or one of your choosing:

God, thank you for bringing us back together to continue this study of the Ten Commandments. Open our hearts and minds to the message that you have for us. Amen.

The Second Commandment (10–15 minutes)

Supplies: Bibles (at least three different translations)

Invite at least three participants to read aloud Exodus 20:4-6, each from a different translation (if you have more translations, you may choose to read it more than three times).

Note any differences you find between the translations, especially in verse 4. Focus especially on the different words for "idol," which may include images, carved images, or graven images.

Discuss:

- What comes to mind when you hear the word *idol*?

- What do you think of when you hear the phrase "carved image" or "graven image"?

Invite a participant to read aloud:

The Israelites' neighbors worshipped many other gods. Often they represented these gods with physical objects such as statues or poles.

Invite four volunteers to read aloud each of the following scriptures. For each scripture, discuss:

- What do these verses say about idols or carved images?
- What, if anything, do these verses mean for us today?

Scriptures

- Exodus 34:11-14
- Leviticus 19:4
- Psalm 135:15-18
- Isaiah 45:20-22

Note: Exodus 34:11-14 refers to sacred pillars and poles. Worshipping stone pillars was common in parts of the ancient Near East (the region where the Israelites lived). Canaanites, neighbors of the ancient Israelites, created and worshipped poles that represented the goddess Asherah.

Iconic (10–15 minutes)

Supplies: devices with internet access, Bibles, pens or pencils, paper

Divide into teams of two or three. Each team should go throughout your church building or meeting space and find all the pictures of Jesus they can. This could include images found on paintings, stained glass windows, sculptures, pictures on the covers of books or Sunday school curriculum, children's drawings, and so forth. Be careful not to disturb other classes, meetings, or activities that are going on at the same time.

One person from each team should write a short description of each image of Jesus on the paper that has been provided.

Spend no more than five minutes looking for pictures of Jesus, then reconvene. Each team should briefly describe the images of Jesus it saw. Then discuss:

- What was similar about the images you saw?
- What made some images unique?
- What do these pictures tell us about Jesus?

Invite a participant to read aloud the following:

> *Because God commanded the people not to make idols or carved images, and because Christians know that Jesus is God in human form, some early Christians felt that any pictures or sculptures of Jesus were entirely off limits. On the other hand, early Christians also developed a tradition of creating icons. Icons are artistic representations of Jesus, Mary, angels, saints, and martyrs. (Martyrs are those who were killed for their faith.) Often icons are paintings, but they also can be carvings, embroideries, or other types of art. The tradition of creating icons and using them in worship for personal devotion continues today, especially in Eastern Orthodox churches. Those who use icons don't worship them. Rather, these works of art help worshippers focus on divine things and remember the great people and moments of the faith.*

Divide into teams of three or four and make sure that each team has a device that can access the internet. Each team should do an image search for "Christian iconography" and should spend a few minutes looking through the icons that come up and finding one icon that is especially interesting.

After a few minutes, each team should show its chosen icon to the group and explain why that icon was particularly interesting. (If resources permit, have each team send a picture of the icon it chose to an adult leader, who can put these images on a slideshow for the entire group to see.)

Then discuss:

- What similarities did you notice among the icons you looked at? What symbols or objects showed up on multiple icons?
- What is the difference between an icon and an idol?

- How can we use icons in worship or in our personal prayers without violating the second commandment?
- Read aloud Exodus 25:17-22. In these verses, God is describing the sacred chest that would contain God's written law. Why did God command the Israelites to decorate the cover of the chest with "winged heavenly creatures"? What, do you think, are these winged heavenly creatures (or what do they represent)?

What Makes an Idol? (10–15 minutes)

Supplies: whiteboard or large sheet of paper, markers, devices with internet access

Discuss:

- Now, what comes to mind when you hear the word *idol*?

Invite a participant to read aloud the following:

> *One of the first things that probably comes to mind when we hear the word* idol *is a celebrity whom we revere or look up to. We talk about "idolizing" entertainers and athletes. Usually, we use this language figuratively. We don't really worship these people as gods; we just respect them and aspire to have similar success and achievements. When we talk about not worshipping idols, we aren't saying that we shouldn't look up to a pop star or basketball player. So what are we talking about?*

To better understand what the second commandment is talking about, discuss:

- What makes God different from, or greater than, an idol?
- How is worshipping God different from worshipping an idol?

Invite a participant to read aloud the following:

> *One of the most significant differences between God and an idol is that we can have a relationship with God. You can't be in a relationship with an idol.*

Divide a whiteboard or large sheet of paper into two columns. Title one column "A relationship..." Title the other "A relationship is not..."

Spend about two minutes coming up with words or phrases to complete the sentence "A relationship...," and list these in the first column. Examples might include, "A relationship grows and changes over time," or "A relationship involves more than one person," or "A relationship can be difficult and frustrating at times."

Then spend about two minutes coming up with words or phrases to complete the sentence "A relationship is not...," and list these in the second column. Examples might include, "A relationship is not one-sided," or "A relationship is not easy," or "A relationship is not self-serving."

Following this activity, discuss:

- Based on what we've written in these two columns, how is having a relationship with God different from worshipping an idol?
- Now that you've had time to reflect on the difference between God and an idol, what are some examples of idols that you might be tempted to worship? In other words, how might you become devoted to people, things, or ideas that you cannot have a relationship with?

Closing (5 minutes)

To close, discuss the following questions:

- What is one thing you learned from our time together today that you didn't know before?
- What is one question you have as a result of what we've discussed today?

Close with the following prayer or one of your choosing:

God, thank you for bringing us together for this time of study and reflection. Thank you for the insights you've given us and the questions you've raised. As we leave here, guide us and strengthen us so that we can invest in our relationship with you. We pray these things in Jesus's name. Amen.

Session 3

"I SWEAR TO GOD!"

> Do not use the Lord your God's name
> as if it were of no significance.
> (Exodus 20:7)

"OMG," whether as just three letters or as the words they represent, is one of our culture's most common expressions of joy, shock, frustration, fear, and anticipation. The "O" stands for "Oh," and the "M" stands for "My." The "G" can stand for different things. Some people say "Goodness." Others say "Gosh." And, of course, for a lot of people the "G" stands for "God."

The third commandment tells us not to use God's name "as if it were of no significance." Other translations say that we shouldn't misuse God's name or that we shouldn't use God's name "in vain." Often this is taken to mean that we should only use the word *God* (or *Jesus* or *Lord*) when we are actually talking to or about God. While saying "Oh my God" as an expression of surprise or excitement is one way of misusing God's name, the third commandment is about more than what we say when we stub our toes or see a trailer for a highly anticipated movie.

Another common way of misusing God's name is by swearing. When someone is really serious about something, that person might say, "I swear to God." This was a problem for the ancient Israelites. When someone swears to God that he or she will do something and then fails to do it, it makes God look bad. The third commandment told the Israelites, "If you're going to swear by God's name, you'd better be true to your word." Jesus would later tell his followers, "You shouldn't really swear at all."

In this session we'll look at swearing and other ways we misuse God's name.

Getting Ready

For this session you will need:

- Bibles (different translations if possible),

- paper and pens or pencils,
- a whiteboard or large sheet of paper,
- markers, and
- devices with internet access.

Opening: Substitute Words (5–10 minutes)

Supplies: a whiteboard or large sheet of paper, markers

As participants arrive, have everyone think about the non-offensive curse words and phrases that they use when they are upset or that fictional characters use when they're upset. This would include words and phrases like "Darn" and "Dang it." It would also include non-swear words from television shows, books, or movies. (SpongeBob SquarePants, for instance, uses a variety of non-offensive curse words such as "Barnacles!" "Tartar Sauce!" and "Fish Paste!")

When most participants are present, work together to make a list of these words and phrases on a whiteboard or large sheet of paper.

Then discuss:

- Why do we use these silly words and phrases?
- Why do we call offensive words and phrases "swear words"? How is saying these words like swearing on something? (It is okay if you have a hard time coming up with answers.)
- Why do we also call offensive words and phrases "curse words"? How is saying these words like cursing someone?

Invite a participant to read aloud the following:

> We use safe words and phrases such as these so that we don't end up saying more offensive words and phrases when we are angry or frustrated. Swearing, or cursing, is a difficult topic. People have different ideas about what words or phrases are bad, and in what situations. But the third commandment helps us better understand how we can be faithful to God through the words we use, and those we don't use.

Open with the following prayer or one of your choosing:

God, thank you for bringing us back together to continue this study of the Ten Commandments. Open our hearts and minds to the message that you have for us. Amen.

The Third Commandment (5 minutes)

Supplies: Bibles (at least several different translations)

Invite at least three people to read aloud Exodus 20:7, each from a different translation.

Discuss any differences you notice between the translations.

Invite a participant to read aloud the following:

> *Many people learn the third commandment as "You shall not take the Lord's name in vain." This language comes from the King James Version, which reads, "Thou shalt not take the name of the Lord thy God in vain." More current translations say that we should not "misuse" or "make wrongful use" of God's name. The Common English Bible, which was completed in 2011, says, "Do not use the Lord your God's name as if it were of no significance."*

Discuss:

- What does it mean to do something "in vain"?
- What, do you think, does it mean to use God's name "in vain"?
- What does it mean to "misuse" or "make wrongful use" of God's name? In what ways might someone misuse God's name?
- What does it mean to use God's name "as if it were of no significance"?
- After considering all of these translations, what do you think God is telling us in this commandment?

OMG! (10 minutes)

Supplies: pens or pencils, paper, devices with internet access

Invite a participant to read aloud the following:

One of the most common ways that people have followed the third commandment is by not saying, "Oh my God," when they are not actually talking about God.

Discuss:

- About how many times in a day (take a guess) do you hear the phrase "Oh my God"?
- Where do you hear this phrase? (on television, from friends, from teachers, and so forth)
- How do you respond to hearing this phrase? Does it bother you? Do you even notice it?
- Are there times when saying "Oh my God" is appropriate? If so, when?

Invite a participant to read aloud the following:

While many people don't worry about saying "Oh my God" when they're surprised or shocked or excited, a lot of people go out of their way not to. They come up with alternatives, such as "Oh my gosh" or "Oh my goodness" to avoid misusing God's name.

Invite each person to come up with his or her own "Oh my..." statement by coming up with a word beginning with G that could be used instead of saying God's name. Write them down on the paper that has been provided.

After a minute or so, allow each person to say his or her "Oh my..." statement.

Then discuss:

- Why does God command us not to use God's name in this way? Why might it be bad to say "Oh my God" to express shock or excitement?
- What does the word *profanity* or *profane* mean? What makes something profanity?

Look up the word *profane* in online dictionaries. Focus especially on the roots of the word and where the word comes from.

Invite a participant to read aloud the following:

The word profane *comes from the Latin words* pro, *meaning "outside," and* fanum, *meaning "temple." To make something profane literally means to take something that is sacred and to use it in a way that is not holy. So using God's name when we're angry or delighted is literally profanity.*

I Swear (10 minutes)

Supplies: Bibles

Discuss:

- What does it mean to swear something? When have you sworn to do, or not do, something?
- Often when people swear, they swear on something or to something. What sorts of things, or people, do people swear on or swear to?

Invite a participant to read aloud the following:

While we shouldn't say "Oh my God" when we aren't addressing God, the main purpose of the third commandment is to keep people from swearing falsely. To swear means to make a serious promise that one vows to uphold. In many ancient cultures, when people made a serious promise or commitment, they would swear to their god, or gods. This was a way of guaranteeing that they would keep their promise. Even today, people say, "I swear to God!" Before testifying in court, many witnesses swear to tell the whole truth, "so help me God."

Invite a volunteer to read aloud each of the following scriptures:

- Leviticus 19:12
- Numbers 30:2

Discuss:

- What is God telling God's people to do, or not to do, in these verses?
- Do these verses say that we can never swear on God's name? Why, or why not?

- Why would it be a problem to falsely swear something in God's name? What effect might that have on our relationship with God?

Jesus: Next Level (10–15 minutes)

Supplies: Bibles

Divide into teams of three or four. Each team should read aloud one of the following scriptures from Jesus's Sermon on the Mount in the Gospel of Matthew and answer the questions below. It is okay if not all scriptures are used or if more than one team uses the same scripture.

Scriptures:

- Matthew 5:21-26
- Matthew 5:27-28
- Matthew 5:38-42
- Matthew 5:43-48

Questions:

- What existing law does Jesus refer to ("You have heard that it was said…")?
- How does Jesus challenge his listeners to do more than what the law says?
- Why does Jesus say that just following the law is not enough?

Allow a few minutes for teams to read and answer the questions. Then each team should summarize its scripture and its answers to the questions.

Discuss:

- What is the common theme in all of these scriptures?
- What do these verses tell us about what Jesus expects from his followers?

Then a volunteer should read aloud Matthew 5:33-37.

Invite a participant to read aloud the following.

As we've seen, the law in the Old Testament says that we shouldn't swear falsely. In other words, it's okay to swear as long as we're true to our word. But, as he does with murder and adultery and retaliation, Jesus holds his followers to a higher standard.

Discuss:

- What does Jesus teach about swearing? (Many translations say "solemn pledges" or "oaths.")
- Why would Jesus not want us to swear at all?
- What do you think Jesus means when he says, "Let your *yes* mean yes, and your *no* mean no" (verse 37)?
- When have you struggled to stay true to your word or to follow through on your promises?

Closing (5 minutes)

To close, discuss the following questions:

- What is one thing you learned from our time together today that you didn't know before?
- What is one question you have as a result of what we've discussed today?

Close with the following prayer or one of your choosing:

God, thank you for bringing us together again for this time of study and reflection. Thank you for the insights you've given us and the questions you've raised. As we leave here, give us the wisdom and courage to be faithful to your name in all that we do. We pray these things in Jesus's name. Amen.

SESSION 4

REDISCOVERING THE JOY OF SABBATH

> Remember the Sabbath day and treat it as holy.
> (Exodus 20:8)

"I can't do that right now, it's the Sabbath" is a great way to get out of doing chores or homework on Sunday. But the fourth commandment, which tells us to remember the Sabbath, is a commandment that a lot of God's followers today either don't take seriously or ignore entirely. We might make time each Sunday for worship and relaxation, but setting aside an entire day each week as a holy day of rest and devotion is further than a lot of people are willing to go.

Yet God considers remembering the Sabbath important enough to make it one of the Ten Commandments. So what's the big deal about the Sabbath? We can answer that question by looking at two of the words in Exodus 20:8. The first is *remember*. The Sabbath is a day to remember what God has done for us and who we are as God's people. The second is *holy*. God calls us, God's people, to be holy, or set apart. One way we do this is by honoring the time that God has set aside for us for rest and worship.

In this session, we'll consider the meaning of Sabbath and what it meant for the ancient Israelites. We'll also look at what this commandment means for followers of Christ today.

Getting Ready

For this session you will need:

- Bibles,
- paper and pens or pencils,
- a whiteboard or large sheet of paper,
- markers, and
- devices with internet access.

Opening: Easy Like Sunday Morning (5–10 minutes)

Supplies: whiteboard or large sheet of paper, markers

On a whiteboard or large sheet of paper, create two columns. At the top of the first column, write "Always on Sunday." At the top of the second column, write "Never on Sunday." As participants arrive, have the group work together to fill the columns with things they do almost every Sunday and things they almost never do on Sunday.

When most participants are present, review your lists together. Then discuss:

- Based on this activity and the lists we made, how is Sunday different from other days of the week?

Invite a participant to read aloud the following:

> *This session is about the fourth commandment, which tells us, "Remember the Sabbath day." While Sunday is the Sabbath day for most Christians, this commandment is about more than how we spend our weekends.*

Open with this prayer or one of your choosing:

God, thank you for bringing us back together to continue this study of the Ten Commandments. Open our hearts and minds to the message that you have for us. Amen.

The Fourth Commandment (5 minutes)

Supplies: Bibles

Invite a volunteer to read aloud Exodus 20:8-12. Then discuss:

- If someone were to ask you, "What does it mean to 'Remember the Sabbath day and treat it as holy'?" what would you say to that person?
- According to these verses, why is the Sabbath day important? Read Genesis 2:2-3 for context.

Word Study: Sabbath (10 minutes)

Supplies: devices with internet access

Discuss:

- What comes to mind when you hear the word *sabbath*?

Divide into pairs or teams of three and make sure that each team has a device with internet access. Each team should look up the word *sabbath*. Teams should answer the questions below.

- What do these definitions say about the origin of the word *sabbath*? (What language or languages does it come from, and what does it mean in these languages?)
- What do these definitions say about when people of different religions observe the Sabbath?

After a few minutes, teams should tell the group their answers to these two questions. Then discuss:

- What, if anything, surprised you about the definitions you looked at? What, if any, new things did you learn?

Don't Forget (15 minutes)

Supplies: Bibles, pens or pencils, paper

Invite volunteers to read aloud each of the following scriptures. As volunteers read, write on a sheet of paper any key words that you hear about the Sabbath and how we are to observe the Sabbath.

Scriptures:

- Exodus 31:12-14
- Deuteronomy 5:12-15
- Isaiah 58:13-14

Ask volunteers to read aloud the key words they identified.
Chances are good that two of the words people identified were *remember* and *holy*. Let's focus on the word *remember*.

Divide into teams of three or four. Teams will have exactly two minutes to list on a sheet of paper people and events that we—as a church, as a culture, or as a country—remember. This could include people whom we celebrate on holidays, important moments in history that we commemorate with statues or ceremonies, or historical moments that shaped how we live today.

After two minutes, teams should take another two minutes to jot down how we remember these people and events. (For example: "with a federal holiday," "by learning a song in elementary school," "by observing a moment of silence on a certain day," and so on.)

Have each team read aloud its list. You might award a small prize to the team that listed the most people and events. (Only count an item on the list if the team was able to say how we remember it.)

Then discuss:

- Why do we go out of our way to remember important people and events?
- Are there people and events that we, as a church or community or culture, don't remember that you think we should? If so, who or what?
- What are we remembering when we remember the Sabbath?

Keep It Holy (10–15 minutes)

Supplies: whiteboard or large sheet of paper, markers, pens or pencils

Discuss:

- What does it mean for something to be holy?
- Whom or what (people, places, events, activities, and so forth) do you consider holy? Why are these people and things holy?

Invite a participant to read aloud the following:

> *The Hebrew word translated as "holy" in the Old Testament is* qadosh, *pronounced ka-DOSH. This word describes things that have been set apart for God. If something is "set apart," it is special or different. When we say that the Sabbath is holy, we say that it is special and different, and we don't treat it like any other day.*

Earlier in this session, you made two lists: a list of things that you always do on Sunday and a list of things that you never do on Sunday. Look back over these lists and work together to underline any items on either list that have something to do with Sunday, the Sabbath, or being holy. Take about a minute to do this.

Then, as a group, divide a whiteboard or large sheet of paper into two columns. Label one column "Should" and the other "Should Not."

In the "Should" column list things that we, as followers of Christ, *should* do on a holy Sabbath day. These don't need to be things that we would do every single Sunday but can also include things such as taking Holy Communion or having dinner with the extended family that people might do only on certain Sundays.

Spend no more than two minutes on the "Should" column; then move on to the "Should Not" column. List in this column things that we should avoid doing on a day we've set aside as a holy day. Draw from some of the scriptures you looked at earlier in the session.

Spend no more than two minutes on the "Should Not" list. Then allow a minute to reflect on how you observe the Sabbath. Do you make an effort to do the things on the "Should" list? Do you avoid the items on the "Should Not" list? What could you do better or differently?

Then discuss:

- What could you do differently to more faithfully observe the Sabbath day?
- What is most difficult about keeping the Sabbath holy?
- Scripture tells us to keep the Sabbath holy by resting and not doing work. What does rest have to do with holiness?

Jesus and the Sabbath (10 minutes)

Supplies: Bibles

Invite a participant to read aloud the following:

> Jesus taught his followers the importance of the law that God had given Moses, including the Ten Commandments. But the way that he understood and applied the commandment to

remember the Sabbath put him at odds with some religious leaders.

Divide into three teams. Assign each team one of the following scriptures. Each team should read its scripture and answer the questions below. (If you have a small number of participants, it is okay if you have only one or two teams and can look at only one or two scriptures.)

Scriptures:

- Matthew 12:9-14
- Mark 2:23-28 (This scripture refers to 1 Samuel 21:1-6.)
- Luke 13:10-17

Questions:

- What does Jesus do on the Sabbath that gets him into trouble with religious leaders?
- How does Jesus respond to his critics?
- What does this story teach us about what it means to keep the Sabbath holy?

Allow about four minutes for reading and discussion; then invite each team to summarize its scripture and its answers to the questions.

A Sabbath State of Mind (10 minutes)

Supplies: pens or pencils, paper

Discuss:

- The Bible has a lot to say about keeping the Sabbath. Why, do you think, is keeping the Sabbath so important?

Invite a participant to read aloud the following:

Setting aside time for Sabbath rest allows us time for worship and devotion. It gives us an opportunity to recharge mentally and spiritually so that we are prepared to handle the work and the challenges that we will face during the rest of the week. And, as we have seen in this session, the Sabbath is a chance for us to remember all that God has done for us.

While the fourth commandment tells us to keep the Sabbath day holy, and while most of the scriptures on the Sabbath deal with a special day of the week, Sabbath rest doesn't have to be limited to one particular day.

Think about your average week. When in your week do you have time for Sabbath rest—time for rest, reflection, and devotion? List these times on a sheet of paper.

Select at least one of these times. Commit this week to setting aside that time for Sabbath rest.

Closing (5 minutes)

To close, discuss the following questions:

- What is one thing you learned from our time together today that you didn't know before?
- What is one question you have as a result of what we've discussed today?

Close with the following prayer or one of your choosing:

God, thank you for bringing us together again for this time of study and reflection. Thank you for the insights you've given us, for the questions you've raised, and for your gift of the Sabbath. As we leave here, give us the strength to be able to set aside time in our busy schedules for rest, reflection, and devotion. We pray these things in Jesus's name. Amen.

Session 5

A QUESTION OF HONOR

Honor your father and your mother.
(Exodus 20:12)

The first four commandments involve how we love, serve, honor, and relate to God. The other six commandments involve how we love, serve, honor, and relate to one another. The first commandment in this second set tells us to "honor" our father and mother.

"Honoring" someone means showing that person respect and making time for that person. In the New Testament, the apostle Paul tells us that honoring our parents involves obeying them. As we mature, become more independent, and have to juggle more responsibilities, making time for our parents and following their instructions becomes more difficult. Even if we love and care for our parents, we might not give them the honor they deserve.

On the other hand, not all parents seem worthy of honor. How do we honor parents who are abusive and neglectful? What responsibility do parents have to their children? And what about the many people who are raised by grandparents, aunts and uncles, and others?

In this session, we'll discuss the answers to these questions and others. We'll look at the meaning of the word *honor* and examine what Scripture teaches us about our relationships with parents and those who play that role in our lives.

Getting Ready

For this session you will need:

- Bibles,
- pens or pencils,
- a whiteboard or large sheet of paper,
- markers,
- devices with internet access, and
- paper.

Words of Life: Youth Study Book

Opening: Common Threads (5–10 minutes)

As participants arrive, look over the first four commandments together and talk about what they have in common. If you need a refresher, these are the first four:

1. "You must have no other gods before me" (Exodus 20:3).
2. "Do not make an idol for yourself" (Exodus 20:4).
3. "Do not use the Lord your God's name as if it were of no significance" (Exodus 20:7).
4. "Remember the Sabbath day and treat it as holy" (Exodus 20:8).

Then invite a participant to read aloud:

We can think of the Ten Commandments as falling into two groups. The first four commandments are one group. In this session, we'll start examining the second group.

Open with this prayer or one of your choosing:

God, thank you for bringing us back together to continue this study of the Ten Commandments. Open our hearts and minds to the message that you have for us. Amen.

Shifting Our Focus (5–10 minutes)

Supplies: Bibles

Ask a volunteer to read aloud Matthew 22:34-40.
Discuss:

- According to Jesus, what are the two greatest commandments?
- What does Jesus say about these commandments in verse 40?

If time permits, look up the following two scriptures, which are the sources of the two commandments Jesus names.

- Deuteronomy 6:4-5
- Leviticus 19:18

Invite a participant to read aloud the following:

Neither of the commandments that Jesus names are from the Ten Commandments. But, in a way, these two laws are a summary of the Ten Commandments—as well as all the other laws in the Old Testament. The first four commandments involve loving God "with all your heart, with all your being, and with all your mind." They instruct us how to make our relationship with God a priority, to turn away from false gods and idols, to respect God with our speech and actions, and to set aside holy time each week. The other six commandments, including the commandment we'll explore in this session, involve loving our neighbor.

The Fifth Commandment (5 minutes)

Supplies: Bibles

A volunteer should read aloud Exodus 20:12 while everyone else follows along.

Then discuss:

- Why do you think honoring one's parents is so important that an entire commandment is devoted to it?
- What does it mean to "honor" one's father and mother?
- What does God promise to those who are faithful to this commandment?

To Honor, or Not to Honor (10 minutes)

Supplies: a whiteboard or large sheet of paper, markers, devices with internet access

Divide a whiteboard or large sheet of paper into two columns. Label one column "Honoring Is..." Label the other column "Honoring Is Not..."

What does it mean to honor someone or something? Brainstorm ideas and list them in the first column. Examples might include "respecting" or "making time for." Take a minute or two to fill in this column.

Consider what it means to dishonor someone or something. Brainstorm ideas and list them in the second column. Examples might include "ignoring" or "gossiping about." Take a minute or two to fill in this column.

Divide participants into teams of three or four. Make sure that each team has a device with internet access. Teams should look up definitions of *honor*. Identify key words from these definitions. Allow a couple minutes for teams to work. Then each team should read aloud the key words it identified and discuss:

- What do these words teach us about what it means to honor someone or something?

Invite a participant to read aloud the following:

> *The Hebrew word translated as "honor" is kavod (pronounced kah-VODE). Kavod literally means "heavy" or "weighty," so in that sense to honor means to give weight to something.*

Discuss:

- What does it mean to "make light" of something?
- What is the opposite of "making light" of something?

Invite a participant to read aloud the following:

> *If we honor someone or something, we take that person or thing seriously. One translation of the third commandment is "Do not use the LORD your God's name as if it were of no significance." To honor is to treat someone or something as if he, she, or it were of great significance.*

Honor and Obey (5 minutes)

Supplies: Bibles

Invite a participant to read aloud Ephesians 6:1-4. The apostle Paul wrote these verses as part of a letter to the church in Ephesus, which is in current-day Turkey.

Discuss:

- Does "honoring" our parents mean that we should obey them? Why, or why not?
- Paul says that children should obey their parents. Why is children obeying parents so important to Paul?
- Are there situations when children should not obey their parents? If so, when? (Don't spend too much time on this question. You will discuss it more in a later activity.)
- What instructions does Paul give to parents?
- What does Paul mean when he says to parents, "Don't provoke your children to anger"?

Worthy of Honor? (10–15 minutes)

Supplies: pens or pencils, paper

Invite a participant to read aloud the following:

Parents are human beings. They make mistakes like anyone else. Many parents, even when they mess up, have their children's best interests at heart. But we know that there are parents who don't. There are parents who hurt or neglect their children. How do we honor parents like this?

Discuss:

- Is there a way to honor parents who are abusive? If so, how?

Invite a participant to read aloud:

Being faithful to the fifth commandment does not mean making excuses for bad and abusive behavior. We know that one understanding of the word honor *is to take seriously and not make light of. We definitely should not make light of parents who have broken and unhealthy relationships with their children. But we also should not expect children to obey parents who would hurt them or put them in unsafe situations.*

Regardless of your relationship with your legal parents or guardians, think about other adults who are like parents to you. This could include an aunt or uncle, a grandparent, a teacher or coach, a pastor, a friend's parent, or any other adult who loves you like you were his or her child. On a sheet of paper, write this person's name and explain why he or she is like a parent to you.

After a couple minutes, volunteers may talk about the people they described.

Then invite a participant to read aloud:

> *The people whom we honor as parents don't always have to be our biological parents or even our legal guardians. They can be any adults in our lives who love us unconditionally, who hold us accountable for our words and actions, who guide and support us, and who are willing to make sacrifices for us. It is important that we recognize, honor, and respect these people.*

On a separate sheet of paper, write a letter to an adult who is important to you but who isn't your biological parent or legal guardian. Thank this person for loving and caring for you, for giving you guidance and discipline, for supporting you, or for anything else he or she has done for you, or all of these things.

Spend a few minutes writing. It is okay if you don't finish the letter during this time. You may finish it later. While you don't have to send the letter to this person, consider doing so, even if you send it at a later date.

Jesus on Honoring Parents (5–10 minutes)

Supplies: Bibles

A volunteer should read aloud Matthew 12:46-50.
Discuss:

- How does Jesus respond when someone mentions his mother and brothers?
- How might Jesus's response relate to our discussion on adults who play a parental role even though they are not our biological or legal parents?

Invite a participant to read aloud the following:

> *After reading these verses, we might get the idea that family relationships don't matter much to Jesus. But elsewhere in*

the Gospels, we see that the fifth commandment is important to Jesus.

Ask a volunteer to read aloud Mark 7:8-13.
Invite a participant to read aloud the following:

The key to understanding what Jesus is talking about is verse 11. When Jesus talks about "corban," he is referring to a vow that the Pharisees had made to donate a certain amount of their wealth and resources to the temple. Jesus suggests that some of these Pharisees used this vow as an excuse not to care for their parents financially. In other words, the Pharisees were saying to their parents, "I would help you out, but I gave all my money to the temple." Jesus is clear that, by making this excuse, the Pharisees are violating the fifth commandment.

Discuss:

- When have you made an excuse to avoid helping out your parents? (For example, maybe you exaggerated how much homework you had to avoid having to watch or pick up a younger sibling.)

Finally, a volunteer should read aloud John 19:25-27.
Invite a participant to read aloud the following:

In these verses, Jesus speaks from the cross to his mother and the "disciple whom he loved." This disciple is a key figure in the Gospel of John and is never mentioned by name. Traditionally, this person is believed to be the apostle John.

Discuss:

- How does Jesus honor his mother in these verses?
- What can you do to care for older adults in the church even if they aren't related to you?

Closing (5 minutes)

To close, discuss the following questions:

- What is one thing you learned from our time together today that you didn't know before?
- What is one question you have as a result of what we've discussed today?

Close with the following prayer or one of your choosing:

God, thank you for bringing us together again for this time of study and reflection. Thank you for the insights you've given us and for the questions you've raised. Thank you for the adults in our lives who love us, care for us, support us, and guide us. As we leave here, open our hearts and minds to ways we can help and care for adults in our community of faith. We pray these things in Jesus's name. Amen.

Session 6

THE TRAGEDY OF VIOLENCE, THE BEAUTY OF MERCY

> Do not kill.
> (Exodus 20:13)

The first five commandments are wordy. God gives a commandment, then follows it with an explanation or a consequence. When we get to the second half of the Ten Commandments, things get shorter. The sixth commandment is just three words: "Do not kill."

"Do not kill" sounds simple enough. Most everyone would agree that murder is bad, and most every society in human history has had a law against it. Yet this seemingly simple rule raises a lot of tough questions: What about killing for self-defense, or in battle? Does this commandment only apply to killing humans? Why does God, in other parts of the Book of Exodus, instruct the Israelites to kill those who violate certain laws or members of neighboring armies? In the New Testament, Jesus tells us that this commandment is about more than killing; he tells us that we also should not insult or show anger toward other people.

In this session, we'll examine the complexities of this three-word commandment. And we'll discuss how this commandment is relevant to those of us who have never even thought about murdering someone.

Getting Ready

For this session you will need:

- Bibles,
- paper and pens or pencils,
- a whiteboard or large sheet of paper,
- markers, and
- devices with internet access.

Opening: Murder Mystery (10 minutes)

When at least a few participants are present, ask one person to think of a fictional character from a movie, book, or television show to be the victim of a fictional murder. This person also should think of a fictional killer, who should also be a character from a movie, book, or television show, but need not be from the same story or series.

Once this person has chosen a victim and a murderer, he or she should say: "_____ was murdered, and I know the culprit."

Other participants should try to identify the killer by asking yes-or-no questions. Allow no more than twenty questions and no more than four guesses.

Repeat this game a few times.

Then invite a participant to read aloud:

> Many of our culture's best-known books, movies, and games involve murder. Murder is also the subject of the sixth commandment and the focus of our session today.

Open with this prayer or one of your choosing:

God, thank you for bringing us back together to continue this study of the Ten Commandments. Open our hearts and minds to the message that you have for us. Amen.

The Sixth Commandment (5 minutes)

Supplies: Bibles

A volunteer should read aloud Exodus 20:13. Unlike the previous few commandments we've looked at, which have come with descriptions or consequences, this commandment is only three words.

Discuss:

- Most of our best translations say, "Do not kill," but some translations say, "Do not murder." What is the difference between the words *kill* and *murder*?
- Is it possible for someone to kill without murdering? If so, how?

Invite a participant to read aloud the following:

On the surface, this commandment seems pretty straightforward. But when we dig in, it gets complicated. For one, elsewhere in the Old Testament, God commands the people to kill animals for food or for rituals. So does this commandment only apply to killing humans? If so, what about killing in self-defense or killing to defend a city from being invaded by a foreign army? Let's wrestle with some of these tough questions.

Justified, or Not? (10–15 minutes)

Supplies: Bibles

Invite a participant to read aloud the following:

God gave the Ten Commandments, including this commandment not to kill, to the Israelite people on Mount Sinai, led by Moses. It turns out that Moses had a history with this commandment.

A volunteer should read aloud Exodus 2:11-15.

Divide into two teams to determine whether Moses was justified in killing the Egyptian. One team will play the role of the defense and will argue that the killing was justified. The other team will play the role of the prosecution and will argue that Moses was wrong to kill the Egyptian. (Some participants will likely be making an argument that they don't agree with. That is okay.)

Give teams a few minutes to prepare their arguments. Then the prosecution should take exactly one minute to make its case. The defense will then get thirty seconds to respond to the prosecution's case.

Then the defense should take exactly one minute to make its case. The prosecution will then get thirty seconds to respond.

Discuss:

- Which side, do you think, has a stronger case? Why?
- If you were on a jury that was deciding Moses's fate, what other information would you want to know?

To further illustrate how "Do not kill" is more complicated than it sounds, read and discuss another scripture passage.

A volunteer should read aloud Exodus 22:1-4 while the rest of the group follows along.

Discuss:

- What do these verses say about whether or not someone is justified in killing a thief?
- While these verses say that there are situations when someone who kills a thief "won't be guilty," would you say that these verses encourage killing? Why, or why not?

In an Ideal World (15 minutes)

Supplies: Bibles, pens or pencils, paper. Markers or colored pencils are optional.

While Scripture shows us that the sixth commandment is complicated and that there are even some situations where killing may be justified, it also gives us a vision of something better.

A volunteer should read aloud Isaiah 2:4. Another volunteer should read aloud Micah 4:3.

Discuss:

- What do you notice about these two scriptures?
- What do these scriptures say about God's vision for God's people?

Isaiah 11 shows us another vision of God's promised future. A volunteer should read aloud Isaiah 11:1-9.

Discuss:

- How does God describe God's promised kingdom to the prophet Isaiah in these verses?
- What do these verses have to do with the sixth commandment, "Do not kill"?

Invite a participant to read aloud the following:

> *These verses from Isaiah show us that God's ultimate hope and promise for the world is peace. In this vision a wolf, which would normally make a meal out of a sheep, lives with a lamb, and a lion, instead of killing and eating a calf, eats with the calf.*

God describes a future where killing—even among animals—is no more.

In the spirit of Isaiah 11:1-9 (and especially verses 6-8), write or draw your own vision of God's future kingdom. You might follow the example in these verses and come up with pairs of animals that normally would never live together peacefully. Or you can identify groups of people who often are at odds with one another, sometimes to the point of violence.

You can describe your vision in writing poetically, as Isaiah does, or in paragraph form, or draw it if you prefer.

Allow about four minutes for everyone to work. Then allow time for volunteers to read or show their visions. (Four minutes might not be enough time to finish. If time permits, set aside some time later in the session so that people can continue working.)

Jesus on Killing (10 minutes)

Supplies: Bibles

Divide into two teams. Assign each team one of the scriptures below. Teams should look up and read their assigned scriptures and answer the corresponding questions. (If your group is especially large, you might need to divide into four teams and assign each scripture to two different teams.)

Scripture 1: Matthew 5:21-26

Questions:

- What does Jesus have to say about killing, or murder?
- How is Jesus's understanding of this commandment different from (or greater than) the three words we see in Exodus 20:13, "Do not kill"?
- Is it possible for us to do what Jesus expects in these verses? Why, or why not?
- How might your life change if you made a real effort to deal with anger and other negative emotions in the way that Jesus describes in these verses?

Scripture 2: Luke 22:47-51 and Luke 23:32-43

Questions:

- How does Jesus respond to the people who arrest him and put him on the cross?
- What can we learn from Jesus about how we should respond to violence?
- How do these scriptures relate to our discussion of the sixth commandment?

After teams have had four or five minutes to work, each team should summarize its scriptures and answers to the questions.

A participant then should read aloud the following:

> *The sixth commandment is short and sounds simple, but as we've seen, applying this commandment can be complicated. As Christians, we should look to the teaching and example of Christ. We should work through anger and grudges, we should resist the temptation to act violently or escalate violent situations, and we should strive to respond to violence with love and forgiveness.*

Closing (5 minutes)

To close, discuss the following questions:

- What is one thing you learned from our time together today that you didn't know before?
- What is one question you have as a result of what we've discussed today?

Close with the following prayer or one of your choosing:

God, thank you for bringing us together again for this time of study and reflection. Thank you for the insights you've given us and for the questions you've raised. Empower us to follow Jesus's teaching and example when we experience anger, violence, or killing. We pray these things in Jesus's name. Amen.

Session 7

FAITHFULNESS IN AN UNFAITHFUL AGE

Do not commit adultery.
(Exodus 20:14)

Like "Do not kill," the seventh commandment is short and to the point. And like "Do not kill," this commandment is more complicated than it appears.

Our culture equates adultery and cheating. You commit adultery when you cheat on a spouse or significant other. The ancient Israelites had a narrower definition of adultery, but it still involved having a relationship with another person's spouse. But Jesus, true to form, teaches us that the seventh commandment is about more than just cheating. We commit adultery whenever we objectify someone.

In this session, we'll look at what it means to "objectify" another person. And we'll examine what the seventh commandment meant for the ancient Israelites and how it applies to us in the twenty-first century.

Getting Ready

For this session you will need:

- Bibles,
- paper and pens or pencils,
- a whiteboard or large sheet of paper,
- markers, and
- devices with internet access.

Opening: Love Triangles (5–10 minutes)

Supplies: pens or pencils, paper

Love triangles are a common plot device in movies and books and on television shows. Maybe a character is tempted to cheat on his or her significant other. Or maybe a character has to choose between two suitors.

As participants arrive, think about fictional love triangles. On a sheet of paper, write several sets of characters from movies, books, plays, or television who are involved in love triangles.

When most people are present, discuss:

- Why are love triangles such a popular plot device in fiction?
- When have you become angry with a fictional character because he or she cheated on a significant other or made a poor relationship choice?

Invite a participant to read aloud the following:

> Our discussion of fictional love triangles might seem like a strange way to start a session, but it actually ties in to the seventh commandment: "Do not commit adultery."

Then open with this prayer or one of your choosing:

God, thank you for bringing us back together to continue this study of the Ten Commandments. Open our hearts and minds to the message that you have for us. Amen.

The Seventh Commandment (10 minutes)

Supplies: Bibles, devices with internet access

Invite a participant to read aloud Exodus 20:14.
Discuss:

- What does it mean to "commit adultery"?

Divide into teams of three or four. Make sure that each team has a device with internet access. Each team should look up definitions of *adultery* and discuss the following questions.

- What recurring words, or key words, do you see in these definitions?
- What, if anything, surprised you about these definitions?

After a few minutes, each team should share its answers to the two questions.

No Joking Matter (15–20 minutes)

Supplies: Bibles

Invite a participant to read aloud the following:

While adultery is a serious matter in the twenty-first century, it isn't illegal in most nations and many popular public figures have been guilty of committing adultery without it doing too much damage to their reputation. For the ancient Israelites in the Old Testament, adultery was a very, very serious matter.

Volunteers should read aloud each of the following scriptures:

Scriptures:

- Leviticus 20:10
- Numbers 5:11-22
- Proverbs 6:32-35

Then discuss:

- What do these scriptures tell us about how seriously the ancient Israelites took the sin of adultery?
- Do you think these laws and views on adultery are unreasonable? Why, or why not?

Invite a participant to read aloud the following:

Even though the Old Testament law makes clear how serious the sin of adultery is and how severe the consequences should be, Israel's greatest king was himself guilty of adultery.

Jesus on Adultery (10–15 minutes)

Supplies: Bibles, pens or pencils, paper

On a separate sheet of paper, fill in the blanks of the sentence below with words of your choosing:

The _____ jumped over the _____.

Volunteers should read aloud their sentences. Then discuss.

- What word is the subject of your sentence?
- What word is the object in your sentence?
- In grammar, what is the difference between an object and a subject?
- What does it mean to "objectify" someone?

Invite a participant to read aloud the following:

In grammar, the subject is the person or thing who acts. The object is the person or thing that is acted upon. The word objectify *literally means to treat someone or something as an object. An object is something that exists for us to use. It's something that we do something to. You can't have a relationship with an object. When we objectify someone, we don't consider that person's feelings or choices, we only think about what we can do to the person or get from the person.*

A volunteer should read aloud Matthew 5:27-28.
Discuss:

- In previous sessions, we've seen Jesus teach his followers not just to obey commandments literally but to hold themselves to a higher standard. What does Jesus teach about holding ourselves to a higher standard when it comes to adultery?
- What does it mean to look "lustfully" at another person?

Invite a participant to read aloud the following:

When Jesus talks about looking "lustfully" at someone, he is talking about objectifying that person. When we look lustfully at someone, we don't look at that person as someone whom we could have a relationship with, but as an object to satisfy our desires.

Discuss:

- Why, do you think, is it wrong to look lustfully at, or objectify, someone?
- Why, do you think, does Jesus consider lusting after someone a type of adultery?

Invite a participant to read aloud the following:

> We typically think of adultery as cheating on a spouse or significant other. Cheating is bad because it violates a person's trust and damages our relationship with that person. Objectifying other people also damages relationships. A person can be hurt by knowing that his or her spouse or significant other is lusting after someone else. And it's impossible for two people to be in a relationship if one person treats the other as an object.

Jesus's standard may seem impossible to live up to, but he has more to say on this subject.

Read aloud John 8:1-11.

Discuss:

- What do the Pharisees plan to do to the woman caught in adultery?
- How does Jesus respond to them?
- Is Jesus okay with the woman committing adultery? What does he say to her?

It's Not Just About Marriage and Lust (10 minutes)

Supplies: Bibles, whiteboard or large sheet of paper

As we've seen, adultery does a great deal of damage to relationships. Obviously, adultery isn't the only way that someone can hurt or betray a person he or she is close to. Brainstorm other ways that we hurt or betray the trust of people we're close to. (Examples could include spreading rumors about someone or stealing from someone.) List these ideas on a whiteboard or large sheet of paper.

A participant should then read aloud the following:

> While the Bible has a lot to say about actual adultery, it also uses adultery as a metaphor to describe how God's people damaged their relationship with God.

Volunteers should read aloud Jeremiah 5:1-9, with each person reading a few verses at a time. In these verses, God is speaking to the people of Judah through the prophet Jeremiah. The people of Judah are descendants of the ancient Israelites who received the Ten Commandments.

Discuss:

- Which of the people is God most upset with? (See verse 5.)
- What does God, through Jeremiah, mean by saying that the powerful people of Judah had "committed adultery" (verse 7)?
- Verse 8 says that these people were "snorting for another's wife." Whom, or what, do you think this verse is talking about?

Invite a participant to read aloud the following:

A marriage is a covenant relationship. Each person takes vows to love, serve, and sacrifice for his or her partner. Our relationship with God is also a covenant relationship. God promises to guide us, protect us, and provide for us, and we promise to devote ourselves to God's will. When we fail to uphold our promise, it hurts our relationship with God, much as adultery would. For this reason, when we reflect on the seventh commandment, we should focus not only on cheating on a spouse or a boyfriend or girlfriend but also on being faithful in all of our relationships, including our relationship with God.

Closing (5 minutes)

To close, discuss the following questions:

- What is one thing you learned from our time together today that you didn't know before?
- What is one question you have as a result of what we've discussed today?

Close with the following prayer or one of your choosing:

God, thank you for bringing us together again for this time of study and reflection. Thank you for the insights you've given us and for the questions you've raised. Give us the strength to resist temptation and be faithful to our relationships and to the promises we make to one another and to you. We pray these things in Jesus's name. Amen.

SESSION 8

WE'RE ALL THIEVES. YES, EVEN YOU.

Do not steal.
(Exodus 20:15)

Do not steal. Do not take what belongs to someone else. Seems straightforward enough. But what about using another person's password to sign in to a streaming service? What about finding money lying on the ground and keeping it instead of turning it in or trying to find its owner?

Laws against stealing are necessary in any functioning society. But as followers of Christ, we need to look at the attitudes and motivations behind stealing. Stealing comes from a desire to have more stuff, either because we value possessions more than relationships or because we struggle to meet our basic needs. Jesus calls us to be grateful and content with what we have but also to be generous with our money and resources, so that others are not desperate to have what they need to survive.

In this session, we'll discuss what does and does not qualify as stealing. And we'll look at how we, as God's people, can eliminate the reasons why we're tempted to steal.

Getting Ready

For this session you will need:

- Bibles,
- paper and pens or pencils,
- a whiteboard or large sheet of paper,
- markers, and
- devices with internet access.

Opening: Catch the Thief (5–10 minutes)

When several participants are present, select one person to be the "thief." Everyone except for the thief should close their eyes. While everyone's eyes are closed, the thief should quietly "steal" one item in the room and quietly place this item just outside the door. The stolen item should be something in plain sight for anyone with open eyes. (In other words, it shouldn't be something that is in a drawer or cabinet or underneath something else.)

After the thief has placed the stolen object outside the room, everyone should open their eyes and guess what was stolen. Repeat this game several times until most participants are present.

Then open with the following prayer or one of your choosing:

God, thank you for bringing us back together to continue this study of the Ten Commandments. Open our hearts and minds to the message that you have for us. Amen.

The Eighth Commandment (5 minutes)

Supplies: Bibles

Invite a volunteer to read aloud Exodus 20:15. It's only three words. Discuss:

- Why do you think this commandment is so important that God includes it in the Ten Commandments?
- How would you define "stealing"?

Is That *Really* Stealing? (10 minutes)

Everyone should stand in the middle of your meeting space. Designate one wall of your meeting space the "Yes, That's Stealing" wall. Designate the opposite wall the "No, That's Not Stealing" wall.

A volunteer should read aloud each of the statements below. Participants should move to one side of the room or the other to indicate whether they think each statement is an example of stealing. Participants don't have to move all the way to one side or another, but can stand somewhere in between. (For instance, maybe a participant thinks a situation is technically stealing but isn't really wrong. She might stand in between but closer to the "Yes, That's Stealing" wall. Or maybe a participant has no idea whether or not a situation is stealing. He might stand in the middle of the room.)

After each situation is read aloud and participants move to their spots, volunteers should explain why they stood where they did.

- finding $20 lying on the floor at a store and keeping it instead of turning it in,
- using another person's password to access a streaming service,
- receiving an extra $10 when the clerk at a store hands you your change and putting the money in your pocket without saying anything,
- watching a movie for free on an unlicensed website instead of paying a rental fee or watching it on a legitimate streaming service,
- cancelling your piano lesson at the last minute so that you can spend time with friends (as a result your teacher, who has scheduled time for the lesson, does not get paid),
- accidentally walking out of a store with an item you didn't pay for and not returning to pay for it,
- borrowing something from a friend and never giving it back, or
- finding a pencil lying on the floor in school and keeping it.

Then discuss:

- For which of these situations were we mostly in agreement?
- For which of these situations did we disagree the most?
- Were there situations that you considered stealing but that you don't consider wrong? If so, which ones, and why do you feel this way?
- Were there situations that you did not consider stealing but that still seem immoral to you? If so, which ones, and why do you feel this way?

What If I Find Someone's Donkey? (5–10 minutes)

Supplies: Bibles

"Do not steal" seems like a simple, straightforward commandment. Most societies throughout history have had laws against shoplifting and robbery, and these laws usually are not controversial. Most people seem to agree that it's wrong to take things that don't belong to us. But, like some of the other commandments, when we look more closely, it gets complicated.

A volunteer should read aloud Exodus 23:4-5. These verses are a part of the law that God gave to Moses and appear just a few chapters after the Ten Commandments.

Discuss:

- What instructions do these verses give to people who find an ox or donkey that has wandered off?
- In the situation described in these verses, whom does the ox or donkey belong to? Why is this important?
- How do the instructions in these verses apply to the situations we looked at in the previous activity?

Note: Exodus 23:5 describes an animal who is stuck or exhausted after carrying a heavy load. When God instructs the people to "set it free," this doesn't mean that they should let the animal run off; it means that they should help the animal by lightening its load.

Jesus on Stealing (15 minutes)

Supplies: Bibles, pens or pencils, paper

Divide into three teams and assign one of the scriptures below to each team. (If you have a small number of participants, divide into two teams and assign the first two scriptures to one team.) Team members may wish to take notes.

Each team should read its assigned scripture, then answer the following two questions:

- How does this scripture relate to the eighth commandment, "Do not steal"?
- How does this scripture apply to the situations we looked at earlier?

(It's important to know that none of these scriptures directly mention stealing.)

Scriptures:

- Matthew 6:19-21, 24
- Matthew 7:12
- Luke 12:15-21

Allow four minutes to work; then invite each team to summarize its scripture and answers to the questions.

Invite a participant to read aloud the following:

> *Jesus, in these verses, doesn't directly talk about stealing, but he talks about the reasons why people steal. People steal when they put possessions ahead of relationships and when they put their desires ahead of the needs and wants of others.*

Briefly revisit the "Is That *Really* Stealing?" activity from earlier with one more situation. (As before, participants should start in the middle of the room and move to one side or another depending on whether they consider that situation to be stealing.)

Situation:

- stealing food when you are hungry and impoverished and don't have the means to buy food

As before, allow volunteers to explain why they stood where they did. Invite a participant to read aloud the following:

> *As we've seen in this session, "Do not steal" is not as simple as it sounds. This is especially true when desperation drives people to take what they need to survive. Can we really condemn someone who steals food to feed their children or who doesn't pay certain bills so that they'll have enough money for rent? Technically, people who steal to meet their basic needs are still stealing. But in these situations, we are as guilty as they are.*

Volunteers should read aloud Matthew 25:31-46.
Discuss:

- What does Jesus teach in this scripture about our responsibility to other people, especially people who are desperate or hurting?
- How does Jesus's teaching relate to our discussion of stealing?

Invite a participant to read aloud:

As we've seen in previous sessions, Jesus holds his followers to a high standard. It's not enough for us to just follow the rules. It's good for us to obey the eighth commandment, "Do not steal." But Jesus expects more from us. He expects us to use our time, resources, money, power, and energy to make sure that everyone's needs are met.

Closing (5 minutes)

To close, discuss the following questions:

- What is one thing you learned from our time together today that you didn't know before?
- What is one question you have as a result of what we've discussed today?

Close with the following prayer or one of your choosing:

God, thank you for bringing us together again for this time of study and reflection. Thank you for the insights you've given us and for the questions you've raised. Today we lift up persons who are desperate and struggling to meet their basic needs; and we lift up those who have been hurt by human trafficking. Empower us to use our time, talents, energy, and resources to ensure that all people have freedom and are able to meet their needs. We pray these things in Jesus's name. Amen.

Session 9

STICKS, STONES, AND THE POWER OF WORDS

Do not testify falsely against your neighbor.
(Exodus 20:16)

In the United States, testifying falsely against someone in a court of law is called perjury, and it is illegal. But the ninth commandment, which tells us not to testify falsely, does not apply only to the legal system. As God's people, we should be truthful in all that we say, especially when we are talking about other people.

Even when we don't intend to lie, we may be guilty of testifying falsely. We might exaggerate or stretch the truth in a way that makes someone else look bad, or we may spread a rumor without verifying whether it is actually true.

In this session, we'll examine what it means to testify and why it is so important that we are honest with our testimony. We'll look at how our testimony affects other people and how it reflects on Christ.

Getting Ready

For this session you will need:

- Bibles,
- paper and pens or pencils,
- a whiteboard or large sheet of paper,
- markers, and
- devices with internet access.

Opening: Question the Witness (10 minutes)

As participants arrive, pair off. Talk with your partner and identify an event that you both remember well. This could include a church retreat or mission trip you both went on, a sporting event you both attended (or even watched on television), a movie you both saw, a school activity you were both a part of, and so on.

Once you've identified an event, take turns naming things that you remember about that event. Listen closely to your partner, and see if you agree with everything she or he says. If your partner describes something differently from how you remember it, say, "I don't remember it that way."

After most participants are present and have had a few minutes to compare their memories, discuss:

- Were you and your partner in agreement about how you remembered the event?
- If not, what did you disagree on?
- Where you disagreed, is it possible you were both right? Is it possible you were both wrong?

People rely a great deal on memory. For much of human history, there was no way to make an audio or a video recording of an event, and most people were unable to write. Those who could write had to rely on people's memories to keep accurate records. Still today, memory plays a major role in our legal system. Witnesses describe their memories of an incident and these memories become evidence for judges and juries. But memories are not always reliable. Two people can remember the same event in very different ways. And, as time passes, our memories can change or disappear altogether. Despite these challenges, Scripture—including the ninth commandment—calls on us to be faithful witnesses.

Open with the following prayer or one of your choosing:

God, thank you for bringing us back together to continue this study of the Ten Commandments. Open our hearts and minds to the message that you have for us. Amen.

The Ninth Commandment (10 minutes)

Supplies: Bibles, pens or pencils, paper

Look up and silently read Exodus 20:16. Then on a sheet of paper, write in your own words what you think this commandment means.

Allow two minutes for everyone to read and write; then have volunteers read aloud what they wrote about the meaning of this commandment. (If participants are using different translations of the Bible, volunteers should read aloud Exodus 20:16 from the translation they're using before reading what they wrote.)

Discuss:

- What similarities did you notice about our explanations of this commandment?
- What differences did you notice?
- The key phrase in this commandment is "testify falsely" (or "bear false witness" or "give false testimony," depending on the translation). What, do you think, does it mean to testify falsely?
- What does the word *testify* (or *witness*) bring to mind?

Invite a participant to read aloud the following:

> *In our culture, we usually associate the words* testify, witness, *and* testimony *with the legal system. Witnesses in a courtroom swear to tell the truth when giving testimony about a case. If they don't tell the truth, they can be charged with perjury or the person on trial could be falsely convicted. The ninth commandment instructs us to be truthful in our testimony regardless of whether we're talking to a priest in ancient Israel or an attorney in an American courtroom. For that matter, this commandment also applies to the testimony we give parents, teachers, friends, and anyone else.*

I Heard a Rumor (10 minutes)

Supplies: Bibles

Pick one person to start a short game. This person should say, "I heard a rumor about _____" and name another person in the group. This person should then come up with a ridiculous rumor about the person he or she named. It is very important that these rumors be silly and in no way personal. (For example, "I heard a rumor about Kaylee. I heard that she could breathe underwater and talk to fish." Or "I heard a rumor about

Amir. I heard that every year during Spring Break, space aliens pick him up and take him to their home planet.")

Continue until everyone has been the subject of a ridiculous rumor. (Make sure to avoid multiple rumors about the same person, unless you have a small group and some extra time.)

Then discuss:

- How big of a problem are rumors, and especially false rumors, at your school or among your friends?
- Why is it tempting to spread rumors?
- Why is it tempting to exaggerate or say things that you know aren't completely true?

Volunteers should read aloud the following scriptures:

- Ephesians 4:25-26, 29-32
- James 3:1-10

Discuss:

- How do these scriptures add to our discussion?

False Testimony in Scripture (10 minutes)

Supplies: Bibles

Volunteers should read aloud 1 Kings 21, the entire chapter. It's a long chapter, and there's a lot going on, so have each person read a few verses or a paragraph. Stop as needed to make sure everyone understands what's happening.

After you've read the entire chapter, discuss:

- What do King Ahab and Queen Jezebel want in this scripture? Whom do they want it from?
- What is Ahab and Jezebel's plan to get the land from Naboth? How is false testimony involved?
- How does God, through the prophet Elijah, respond to what Ahab and Jezebel have done?
- What does Scripture say about Ahab and Jezebel's legacy?

This story is an example of someone breaking the ninth commandment. Other scriptures show how God's people took this commandment seriously.

Volunteers should read aloud each of the following scriptures. Briefly discuss what each one has to say about honest testimony.

- Deuteronomy 19:15-20
- Matthew 18:15-20

Jesus and the Ninth Commandment (10 minutes)

Supplies: Bibles

Volunteers should read aloud each of the following scriptures:

- Luke 8:16-17
- Luke 16:10

Discuss:

- What do these verses teach us about being honest and not "testifying falsely"?

Then volunteers should read aloud Matthew 26:59-68, with each person reading a couple verses at a time.

Discuss:

- What role do false witnesses play in this story?
- Why were the chief priests looking for false witnesses?
- Were the priests able to find any false witnesses?
- What testimony did they use to condemn Jesus?
- How did Jesus respond?

Then a volunteer should read aloud John 2:19-22.

Invite a participant to read aloud the following:

> *While religious leaders were willing to use false testimony to convict Jesus, the witness whose words condemned Jesus was actually telling the truth. Jesus did talk about the destruction of the temple and raising it up in three days.*

Discuss:

- What was Jesus talking about when he talked about destroying the temple and raising it up?
- How was the honest testimony at Jesus's trial misunderstood?

Do Not Lie, Ever? (10 minutes)

Supplies: Bibles

Divide into teams of three or four. Each team should discuss the question:

- Are there situations where it is okay to lie?

If a team answers yes, that team should come up with a specific situation where lying would be justified.

If a team answers no, that team should then come up with an answer to the question, "Why is it wrong to lie even when someone's life or safety is at risk?"

Allow a few minutes for discussion. Then each team should summarize what it discussed and, if the team answered yes, explain its situation.

After each team presents either its answers or situation, volunteers should say whether or not they agree with the team's reasoning and why.

A volunteer should read aloud Joshua 2:1-7; 6:17, 25. Another should read aloud Exodus 1:15-21.

Discuss:

- How do these scriptures relate to our discussion?

Invite a participant to read aloud the following:

> *While most people would agree that it is wrong to lie, there seem to be situations where lying is justified. There is no easy answer to the question of whether it is ever okay to lie, but here's something to consider: the ninth commandment says that we should not testify falsely "against [our] neighbor." Rahab and the Egyptian midwives gave false testimony, but they did it out of love for their neighbor.*

Closing (5 minutes)

To close, discuss the following questions:

- What is one thing you learned from our time together today that you didn't know before?
- What is one question you have as a result of what we've discussed today?

Close with the following prayer or one of your choosing:

God, thank you for bringing us together again for this time of study and reflection. Thank you for the insights you've given us and for the questions you've raised. Give us the courage to give honest testimony and to use our words to build people up and to proclaim love for you and your children. We pray these things in Jesus's name. Amen.

Session 10

KEEPING UP WITH THE JONESES

> Do not desire and try to take your neighbor's house. Do not desire and try to take your neighbor's wife, male or female servant, ox, donkey, or anything else that belongs to your neighbor.
> (Exodus 20:17)

The tenth and final commandment is loaded with people and things that we should not desire, or covet. There is so much going on in this verse that some Christian traditions break it into two separate commandments. (These traditions combine the first two commandments so that there are still ten.)

The verse above, taken from the Common English Bible, uses the words "desire and try to take." Many other translations use one word: *covet*. In either case, this commandment is telling us that we should not crave or be envious of other people's possessions and relationships. The examples it gives seem old-fashioned: it says "wife," but not "husband"; it refers to servants; not many people nowadays keep oxen and donkeys. But if we examine what this verse meant to the ancient Israelites, we can apply it to our lives in the twenty-first century.

In this session, we'll look at the problems that arise from desire, or covetousness. We'll also discuss the importance of being content with the blessings God has given us.

Getting Ready

For this session you will need:

- Bibles,
- paper and pens or pencils,
- a whiteboard or large sheet of paper,

- markers, and
- devices with internet access.

Opening: I Want It! Who's Got It? (5–10 minutes)

As participants arrive, they should think about some material possession that they don't have, but really, really want.

When most people are present, participants should take turns saying, "I want _____. Who's got one?" filling in the blank with the name of what they really want. Anyone who owns this particular item should respond, "I have one."

For example, "I want a car. Who's got one?"

When everyone has had a chance to participate, discuss:

- Does it make it easier or harder to really want something when someone you know already has it? Why?

Then open with the following prayer or one of your choosing:

God, thank you for bringing us back together to continue this study of the Ten Commandments. Open our hearts and minds to the message that you have for us. Amen.

The Tenth Commandment (5 minutes)

Supplies: Bibles. Devices with internet access are optional.

A volunteer should read aloud Exodus 20:17, if possible from different translations of the Bible.

Discuss:

- What does it mean to "covet" in this verse? (**Note:** The Common English Bible translation uses the words *desire* and *try to take*. Many other translations use the word *covet*.) If possible, look up *covet* in online dictionaries.
- What specific things does this commandment tell us not to covet or desire? (The list of things not to covet is a bit outdated; we'll examine that later in the next activity.)

That Sounds Old-fashioned (15 minutes)

Supplies: Bibles, pens or pencils, paper

- What about Exodus 20:17 seems outdated or old-fashioned?

Individually or in pairs, write an updated version of this commandment on a sheet of paper. Use the notes below to help you.

- **Do not desire your neighbor's house:** This part of the verse still applies today.
- **Do not desire and try to take your neighbor's wife:** This commandment was given to a culture that believed that wives belonged to their husbands. Only someone who belongs to someone else can be "taken." It was also a patriarchal culture where men were in charge. Thus, this commandment is written specifically to men. Our culture considers marriage an equal partnership of two people in a covenant relationship with each other. And we believe that God's message should be available to all people.
- **…male or female servant:** For the ancient Israelites, servants belonged to their masters. Obviously, we now reject the idea that one human can own another human. But servants in ancient cultures also signified wealth and power, which are still things that many people desire today.
- **…ox, donkey:** In ancient agricultural societies, animals such as oxen and donkeys were technology. They gave people a more efficient means of working their land and transporting goods. While oxen and donkeys are no longer cutting-edge technology (and aren't usually kept as pets), there are plenty of tools, gadgets, and devices that serve similar purposes today.
- **…or anything else that belongs to your neighbor:** This one is open-ended and can apply to anything not covered by the rest of the commandment.

After about five minutes, allow volunteers (whether individuals or pairs) to read aloud their versions of this verse.

Discuss:

- How did this activity help you better understand this commandment?

Covet? (5–10 minutes)

Supplies: paper, pens or pencils, devices with internet access

On a sheet of paper, take one minute to write a definition (in your own words) of the word *covet*. It is okay if you aren't familiar with the word and don't know what it means. It is also okay if you have a good idea of what the word means.

After a minute, each person should read aloud his or her definition.

Then someone with a device with internet access should look up *covet* in an online dictionary and read the definition. See which person's definition is closest to the dictionary definition.

Then discuss:

- While the most common translation of this verse tells us not to covet, the Hebrew also can be translated as "Do not desire and try to take." What does it mean to desire something or someone to the point of trying to take it for yourself?
- Another translation that could be used is *crave*. What does it mean to crave something?
- Why, do you think, does God instruct us not to covet or desire or crave other people's belongings and relationships?

You Can't Have It (15 minutes)

Supplies: Bibles

Divide into teams of three or four. Each team should come up with a short skit of a situation where someone is told that he or she cannot have something and, as a result, wants that thing more than ever. This might involve a parent telling a child that she can't have a certain snack, a teacher telling a student that he can't bring something into the classroom, and so forth.

Allow about four minutes to work, then ask each team to present its skit.

Then discuss:

- When have you, like the people in these skits, wanted something because you were told you couldn't have it?

This tendency to want what we cannot or should not have goes back to the very beginning of Scripture.

Volunteers should read aloud Genesis 2:4-9, 15-16; 3:1-11, with each person reading a few verses at a time.

Discuss:

- While both the man and the woman were tempted by someone else to eat the fruit, neither of them put up much of a fight. Why do you think the man and woman gave in so easily to eating the fruit?
- What made the fruit so desirable?

Jesus on Coveting (10 minutes)

Supplies: Bibles, pens or pencils, paper

A volunteer should read aloud Luke 12:15-21.
Discuss:

- What does this scripture have to do with coveting?
- What, do you think, does the man in Jesus's parable covet?

On a sheet of paper, write or draw about a time when you really wanted something and then, when you finally got it, discovered that you didn't really want or need it after all.

- Is there something in your closet or on a shelf that you saved up for and then didn't end up using?
- Is there a gift you requested for Christmas or a birthday that ended up not being so great?
- Is there a movie or video game that you'd looked forward to for months that turned out to be a disappointment?

Allow a few minutes for everyone to write or draw. Then invite volunteers to read aloud their examples.

A participant should then read aloud the following:

> *The man in Jesus's parable always wants more and is never satisfied. Jesus doesn't say anything about the man coveting other people's wealth, but the man seems to be concerned only with having* more stuff, not with *using it. As a result, he misses opportunities to use his blessings to bless others. When we covet, we stop thinking about what we have and how we are blessed and we focus instead on what we don't have and what we can get.*

Good Desire, Bad Desire (10 minutes)

Supplies: whiteboard or large sheet of paper and markers

Discuss:

- In this session we've looked at a few different words used to translate the Hebrew in the tenth commandment. We've used the words *covet*, *desire*, and *crave*. Is it always wrong to crave or desire something?

Invite a participant to read aloud the following:

> *Desire isn't necessarily bad. For example, it's good for us to desire strong relationships with family, or peace in our nation and world. Here are a few rules of thumb for when desire can become harmful.*

We break the tenth commandment when we...

- ...desire what belongs to someone else, to the point that we would try to take it from them;
- ...become obsessed with having something we shouldn't have or something that will hurt us or others;
- ...become so obsessed with something we want that it becomes more important to us than God;

- ...spend so much money on things that we crave that we don't have money to spend on what is important or to give to the church or people in need.

Divide a whiteboard or large sheet of paper into two columns. Label one column "OK," and label the other "Not OK."

Using these guidelines brainstorm examples of when it is okay to desire or crave something. List these in the "OK" column.

After a couple minutes, brainstorm examples of when it is not okay to desire or crave something. List these in the "Not OK" column.

Thanks for What I've Already Got (5–10 minutes)

Supplies: Bibles, whiteboard or large sheet of paper, markers

Often we are guilty of coveting what others have when we aren't content with what we have.

A volunteer should read aloud 1 Timothy 6:5-10.

Discuss:

- How does this scripture relate to our discussion of coveting and desire?

Paul, in this letter to Timothy, encourages Christians to be happy, or content, with what they already have. This doesn't mean it is okay for people to be hungry or stuck in poverty. But it does mean that each of us has been blessed and that we should focus on these blessings and how we can put them to use instead of worrying about what we don't have or how we can get more.

As a group, work together to list ways in which you are blessed. This can include essentials such as food and shelter, possessions that mean a lot to you, relationships with friends and family, opportunities to learn or participate in activities, and so on. Write these down on a whiteboard or large sheet of paper.

Take a couple minutes to list these blessings. Then invite each person to select three things from the list that are especially meaningful, which apply to them personally. Spend some time in silence thinking about ways you can use each of these blessings to serve God or others. For example, if you are blessed with the ability and opportunity to play the piano, maybe you could use this talent in worship. If you are blessed with good health, maybe you could use this blessing to assist a neighbor who is physically unable to do yard work or household tasks. And, while it might be weird to think of a video game console as a blessing, playing video games could give you an opportunity to connect with a sibling or to comfort a friend who's having a rough time.

After another couple minutes, allow volunteers to name some of the blessings they identified and how they can use these to serve God and others.

Finally, allow an additional period of silence, during which each person should offer a short prayer of thanksgiving for all the ways that God has blessed that person. Say to the participants: "Remember and repeat this prayer whenever you are tempted to covet something that belongs to someone else or that you don't need."

Closing (5 minutes)

To close, discuss the following questions:

- What is one thing you learned from our time together today that you didn't know before?
- What is one question you have as a result of what we've discussed today?

Close with the following prayer or one of your choosing:

God, thank you for bringing us together for this time of study and reflection. Thank you for the insights you've given us and for the questions you've raised. Thank you for all the ways that we have been blessed and for all the opportunities you give us to use these blessings to serve you and your children. In the days and weeks ahead, remind us of what we've learned about your law and your will for us. We pray these things in Jesus's name. Amen.

www.ingramcontent.com/pod-product-compliance
Lightning Source LLC
Chambersburg PA
CBHW021320110426
42743CB00050B/3431